D0752060

ANDREW CLEMENTS

The Handiest Things in the World

Photographs by Raquel Jaramillo

HOUGHTON MIFFLIN HARCOURT
School Publishers

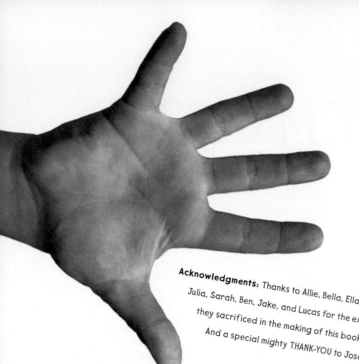

For John and Kristen
—A. C.

For Russell, who makes all things possible
—R. J.

Acknowledgments: Thanks to Allie, Bella, Ella, Jessie, Raimi, Carter, Marshall, Brody, Elise, Marco, Callie, Owen, Taylor, Nate, Julia, Sarah, Ben, Jake, and Lucas for the exquisite use of their hands—and to their moms and dads for the many lovely weekends they sacrificed in the making of this book. A million thanks to Caleb, for being the world's best photographer's assistant. And a special mighty THANK-YOU to Josey, without whose small, beautiful hands this book could not have been made. —R.J.

Acknowledgments

The Handiest Things in the World by Andrew Clements. Photographs by Raquel Jaramillo. Text copyright © 2010 by Andrew Clements. Photographs copyright © 2010 by Raquel Jaramillo. Reprinted by permission of Simon & Schuster Books For Young Readers, an imprint of Simon & Schuster Children's Publishing Division.

Credits

Illustration
40–44 Sonja Lamut.

Printed in China

Little Big Book ISBN: 978-0-547-88480-6
Big Book ISBN: 978-0-547-88473-8

7 8 9 10   0940   21 20 19 18 17 16 15 14

4500498655   A B C D E F G

Table of Contents

Paired Selections

Of all the handy things there are,

the hand itself is best by far.

To grab, to hold, to pull or twist—

the hand itself is handiest.

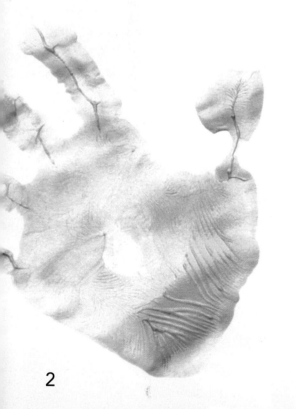

But other things are handy, too.

Just look around, you'll see it's true.

Which things are handiest for you?

Depends on what you need to do.

2

The things I want to show you here—
things old and new, from far and near—
they all came from a simple plan.
The hand is where they all began.

3

Mealtime happens every day.

Keep your fingers clean this way.

Don't let Rover stray away.

This will hold him night and day.

. . . five, six, seven, eight, nine, ten.

Add, subtract, then add again.

Zig-zag,
　　flit-flap—
hard to get.

Catch him with your handy net.

Two wet hands
can hold
and pour.

This will pour a whole lot more.

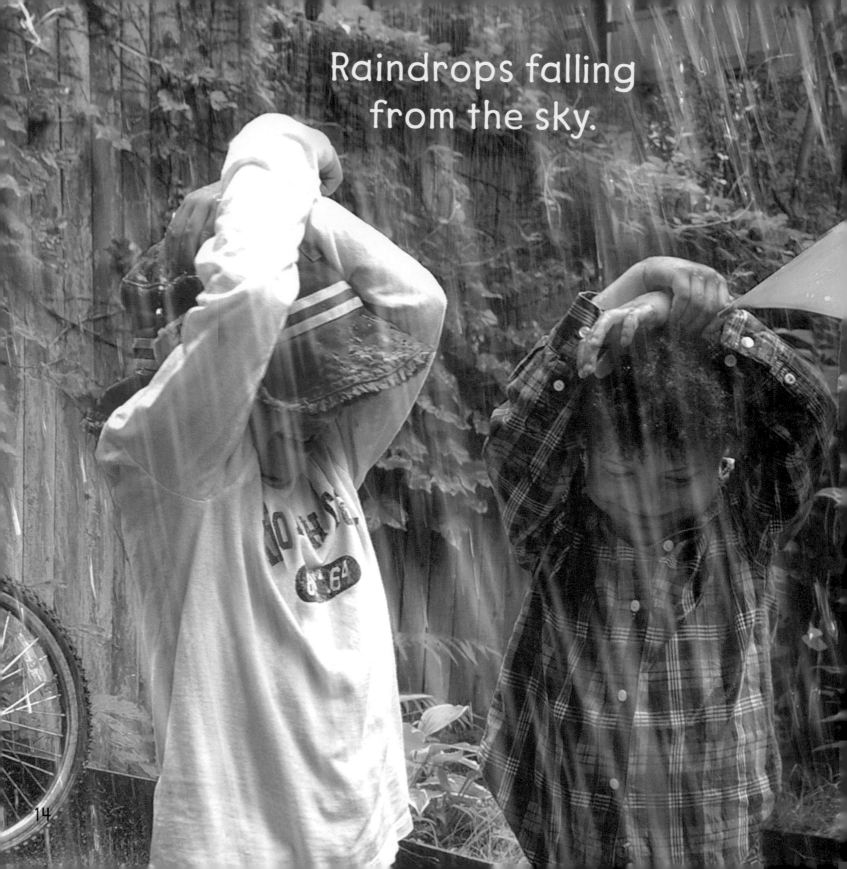

Raindrops falling from the sky.

14

This will help to keep you dry.

Wish I might, wish I may . . .

sweep
this dusty stuff
away.

Handmade
shade
for
squinty
eyes.

18

This
will help
with
sunny
skies.

Digging in and scooping down.

Let's move lots of dirt around.

Tidy
is the way
to be.

22

This will help enormously.

Flap
a hand
to make a
breeze.

24

Push more air
with
one of these.

Tap in rhythm,
keep
the
beat.

Work with these and make some heat.

What's the width,
or length, or height?

28

This
thing
always
gets
it right.

Sticky fingers make a mess.

Mixers make the mess much less.

31

Waves
will
wash
these
words

AWAY

Write
this way,
and words
will

When windy wintertime appears . . .

34

these feel
good on
frosty ears.

Ten thousand years have come and gone . . .

our hands keep working, on and on.
And as the future years unfold,
new handy tools will grip or hold.

Whatever we may need to do,
one fact remains forever true:
For sharing love with tenderness . . .

the hand itself

is handiest.

STONE SOUP

A Tale from Eastern Europe

Long ago, the people in one village had very little food. They didn't have enough food to share with their neighbors.

One day a traveler appeared in the village square. The traveler asked each villager, "Please, may I have some food? I have not eaten for many days." But the villagers said they had no food to share.

Finally the traveler said, "In that case, I will teach you how to make soup from a stone." He took a small stone from his pocket.

"Soup from a stone? Impossible!" said the
villagers. But they were very curious.

"First we will heat a large pot of water over the
fire," said the traveler. He dropped his stone into
the pot. The water boiled and bubbled.

The traveler tasted the soup. "Mmm . . . delicious!" he said. "A pinch of salt and some parsley would make it taste even better, though."

"I think I can find a little salt and some parsley," said a woman. She hurried off, came right back, and put the salt and the parsley into the pot. The soup boiled and bubbled.

The traveler tasted the soup again. "Mmm . . . delicious!" he said. "A cabbage and some potatoes would make it taste even better, though."

"I think I can find a cabbage and some potatoes," said a man. He hurried off, came right back, and put the cabbage and the potatoes into the pot. The soup boiled and bubbled.

The traveler tasted the soup again. "Mmm . . . delicious!" he said. "A few carrots and some chicken would make it taste even better, though."

43

"I think I can find a few carrots and some chicken," said a woman. She hurried off, came right back, and put the carrots and the chicken into the pot. The soup boiled and bubbled.

One by one, the other villagers added things to the pot of stone soup. Others brought bread and good things to drink.

All the people gathered in the village square and shared a delicious feast.

Soon it was time for the traveler to leave. "What a wonderful soup we made from one small stone," he said. "Each one shared just a little, but together we made a feast for us all!"